TALES OF INVENTION

THE
SUBMARINE

Richard and Louise Spilsbury

Heinemann Library

Chicago, Illinois

www.heinemannraintree.com
Visit our website to find out
more information about
Heinemann-Raintree books.

To order:
☎ Phone 888-454-2279
⌨ Visit www.heinemannraintree.com
to browse our catalog and order online.

Edited by Louise Galpine and Laura Knowles
Designed by Philippa Jenkins
Original illustrations © Capstone Global Library Ltd 2011
Illustrated by KJA-artists.com
Picture research by Mica Brancic

Originated by Capstone Global Library Ltd
Printed and bound in China by CTPS

15 14 13 12 11
10 9 8 7 6 5 4 3 2 1

Library of Congress Cataloging-in-Publication Data
Spilsbury, Richard, 1963-
   The submarine / Richard and Louise Spilsbury. -- 1st ed.
   p. cm. -- (Tales of invention)
   Includes bibliographical references and index.
   ISBN 978-1-4329-3831-4 (hc) -- ISBN 978-1-4329-3838-
3 (pb) 1. Submarines (Ships)--Juvenile literature. I.
Spilsbury, Louise. II. Title.
   V857.S67 2011
   623.82'05--dc22
                                            2009049150

9251

Acknowledgments
The author and publisher are grateful to the
following for permission to reproduce copyright
material: Alamy pp. **6** (© LondonPhotos - Homer Sykes),
17 (© Tara Carlin); Corbis pp. **19** (© Bettmann), **23**
(© Bettmann); Getty Images pp. **5** (MPI/Hulton
Archive), **11** (MPI/Hulton Archive), **12** (De Agostini),
13 (Stock Montage/Hulton Archive), **15** (Hulton
Archive), **21** (National Geographic/Emory Kristof), **22**
(National Geographic/Emory Kristof), **26** (Photo by BAE
Systems), **27**; iStockphoto p. **4** (© Christophe Schmid);
© Mary Evans Picture Library 2007 p. **8**; NavSource Naval
History p. **18** (U.S. Navy photo courtesy of Darryl Baker.
Negative scanned courtesy of By Design, Benicia, CA);
NOAA p. **25** (Institute for Exploration/University of
Rhode Island); Photolibrary pp. **10** (North Wind Picture
Archives), **20** (Brand X Pictures); Rex Features p. **7**
(Roger-Viollet), www.navy.mil p. **14** (U.S. Navy, Chief of
Naval Operations Submarine Warfare Division [N87]).

Cover photographs of a diver in a submarine/submersible
reproduced with permission of Corbis/© Stephen Frink
and John P. Holland standing in the conning tower of
his submarine, *Holland VI*, April 1898, Perth Amboy,
New Jersey, reproduced with permission of Corbis/
© Bettmann.

We would like to thank Ian Graham for his invaluable
help in the preparation of this book.

Every effort has been made to contact copyright holders
of material reproduced in this book. Any omissions will
be rectified in subsequent printings if notice is given to
the publisher.

CONTENTS

Look for these boxes

Biographies

These boxes tell you about the life of inventors, the dates when they lived, and their important discoveries.

Setbacks

Here we tell you about the experiments that didn't work, the failures, and the accidents.

EUREKA!

These boxes tell you about important events and discoveries, and what inspired them.

Any words appearing in the text in bold, **like this**, are explained in the glossary.

TIMELINE

2010—The timeline shows you when important discoveries and inventions were made.

BEFORE SUBMARINES

Submarines are special boats that travel underwater. Before submarines were invented, people did not know much about the world deep below the ocean's surface. They dived in shallow water to explore and to find things such as shells and treasure.

People need to breathe in **oxygen** from air to stay alive. Divers held their breath or carried sacks full of air underwater. The air did not last long, which meant divers needed to return to the surface often to breathe in more air. People could stay underwater longer when they breathed in air from the surface through hollow reeds, which were like straws. These were the first **snorkels**.

Divers with snorkels can only breathe underwater when they are close to the surface.

around 3000 BCE—Greek divers use hollow straws to breathe while underwater

3000 BCE   2000 BCE   1000 BCE

Diving bells

Diving bells were heavy containers made of metal, wood, or glass that people used to go underwater. An object floats in water when the upward push on it from the water (called **upthrust**) is greater than the downward force of the object's weight. Diving bells sank because the downward force of their weight was greater than the upthrust. The bell trapped a big bubble of air so people inside it could breathe.

Here a diving bell helps people to find items from a shipwreck in 1752.

EUREKA!

The Greek king Alexander the Great used a glass diving bell in 332 BCE. There is a legend that he saw a sea monster that was so big it took days to swim past the bell!

332 BCE—Alexander the Great uses a diving bell

1578 CE—William Bourne publishes a book called *Inventions or Devices*. It contains his ideas for how to make a working submarine.

0

1000 CE

THE FIRST SUBMARINES

It took the efforts of many different inventors over hundreds of years to develop the submarines we know today. One of the earliest problems inventors solved was making a submarine **watertight**. If water filled the submarine, the people inside it might drown.

The *Drebbel*

Cornelis Drebbel invented the first submarine in 1620. People thought it looked like two wooden rowboats, one stuck on top of the other. It had a short tower on top, with a door for people to get in and out. People inside rowed the machine along using oars through the sides. The whole machine was covered with greased leather to stop water from getting in any gaps, but it was probably still damp inside.

This is a model of the *Drebbel*. It was similar in shape to some modern submarines, but it would have been far less comfortable inside.

EUREKA!

Drebbel continued to improve his inventions. His third submarine was his biggest. Thousands of people stood on the banks of the Thames River in London, England, when Drebbel's submarine took its first public voyage in 1623. The submarine slowly carried 16 passengers a few feet below the river's surface. It stayed underwater for about three hours.

6

1620—The *Drebbel* is the first successful submarine

1600   1610   1620

Cornelis Drebbel (1572–1633)

Cornelis Drebbel was a Dutch inventor who worked for King James I of England. He used ideas of the British inventor William Bourne to help invent his successful submarine. In addition to his submarine, Drebbel invented many other things, including a microscope and a machine that told the time, date, and season.

1634—A French priest and scientist named Marin Mersenne writes that submarines should be made of copper and shaped like long cylinders to move easily through the water

1630   1640

Ups and downs

Drebbel is said to have put heavy weights inside his submarine to make it sink. Making an object heavier in relation to its size or **volume** increases its **density**. There is more **upthrust** on a hollow metal boat than on a solid ball of metal of the same weight because its density is lower. Drebbel could only make his submarine rise by getting rid of the weights to lower its density.

EUREKA!

In 1680 Italian inventor Giovanni Borelli invented **ballast tanks** so his submarine could rise and fall. He wrote about filling goatskin bags inside the submarine with water from outside to increase the submarine's density and make it sink. Then the water would be squeezed out of the bags to lower the submarine's density and make it rise.

This drawing from 1683 shows the ballast tanks inside Borelli's submarine.

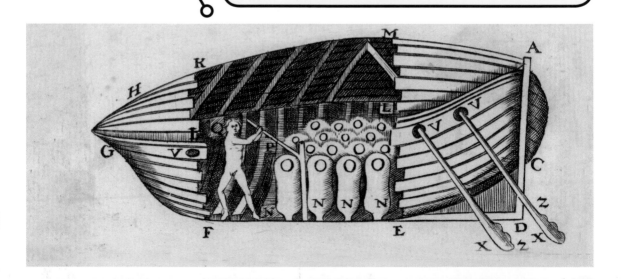

1653—The *Rotterdam Boat* is invented but never works

The carpenter's submarine

The English carpenter Nathaniel Symons invented a submarine with a changing volume in 1729. He sat inside and turned a handle to pull the two halves of the submarine together or spread them apart. When the halves were spread apart, the submarine rose up in the water because it had a bigger volume, and so it was less dense. When the halves were pushed together again, the submarine sank because it had a smaller volume and a greater density.

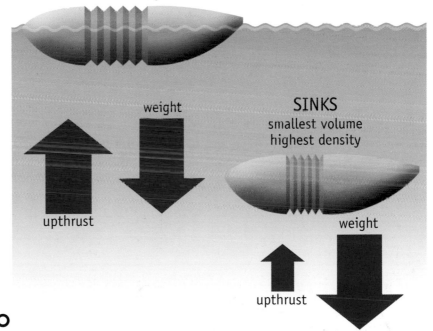

FLOATS
biggest volume
lowest density

weight

upthrust

SINKS
smallest volume
highest density

weight

upthrust

The red arrows in this diagram show how a submarine's volume affects how much upthrust is pushing on it and whether the submarine sinks or rises in the water, even though its weight stays the same.

Sneaking up on the enemy

As submarines improved, governments of different countries realized they could use them to sneak up and attack their enemies. In 1653 the French inventor De Son made the *Rotterdam Boat* for the Belgian navy. They planned to use it to ram holes in British navy ships. Unfortunately, it was too heavy to be moved by the sailors inside it!

The *Rotterdam Boat* was the first submarine designed to attack enemy warships, such as these.

10

1680—Giovanni Borelli invents the ballast tank to change the weight and **density** of a submarine

1680   1690   1700

The *Turtle*

The *Turtle* was the first submarine to attack an enemy warship. This wooden, egg-shaped machine was invented by the American David Bushnell in 1776, during the Revolutionary War. The *Turtle* could move underwater toward enemy British ships, drill holes in their bottoms, and attach clockwork **mines** to blow them up.

It was very cramped inside the *Turtle* submarine. There were handles and foot pedals to spin the **propellers**, move the **rudder** outside, and to fill or empty the **ballast tanks**. Because it was such hard work to operate everything at once, the *Turtle* could only move very slowly.

The *Turtle* got its name because its curved shape looked like a turtle's shell. This 1776 illustration shows what it looked like inside.

Setbacks

On September 6, 1776, U.S. Sergeant Lee moved the *Turtle* next to a British ship called the *Eagle* in New York harbor. He tried to drill a hole in the ship but failed to attach the mine. Lee ran out of air and had to come to the surface, where the enemy chased him off.

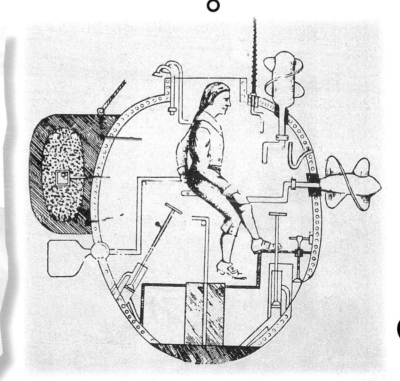

11

IMPROVING SUBMARINES

When a submarine moves through water, **drag** slows it down. Drag is the push of water you can feel when you swim in a pool. A submarine can move faster if it has a smooth, **streamlined** shape because water flows more easily past it, reducing the amount of drag.

The *Nautilus*

In 1797 Robert Fulton designed a new submarine with a streamlined, metal body that would allow it to attack enemies faster. The *Nautilus* had a sail so that it could use wind to move on the water's surface. The sail folded down once the *Nautilus* dived, so it did not increase drag underwater. To move underwater, a handle was turned on the inside to work a **propeller** outside.

The *Nautilus* was designed to move more quickly through water than earlier submarines.

fold-down sail

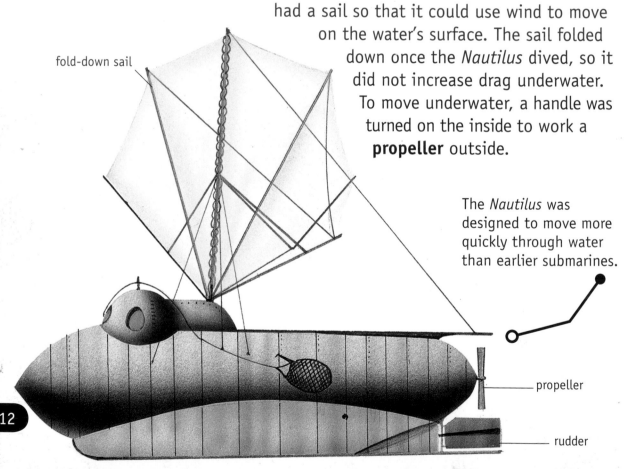

propeller

rudder

1729—Nathaniel Symons builds a submarine that can change its **volume**

Robert Fulton (1765–1815)

U.S. artist Robert Fulton was only a teenager when he made paddle wheels to move a fishing boat on water. Soon he became fascinated by the idea of a "plunging boat." In 1800 Fulton paid to have the *Nautilus* built. He hoped the French government would buy it to use in their war against Britain. The French first thought fighting with submarines was cowardly, but they were impressed with Fulton's submarine in trials. When the *Nautilus* was used in a real attack, it was too slow to catch a British ship. Fulton broke his submarine up and moved on to inventing steamships instead.

Breathing problems

When we breathe in air to get **oxygen**, we breathe out **carbon dioxide**. This gas is poisonous if you breathe too much in. The first submarines could not stay underwater for long because carbon dioxide built up inside them. They could only stay underwater for a long time if the submarine stayed near the surface so the crew could take in fresh air through **snorkels**.

In 1861 Brutus de Villeroi invented the USS *Alligator*. This was the first submarine with a system for keeping the air fresh. Pumping air through a bottle of special liquid removed the carbon dioxide.

The USS *Alligator* was 4 meters (47 feet) long.
Like today's submarines, it had a **streamlined**
shape and an air-cleaning system.

1776—David Bushnell
invents and demonstrates
his *Turtle* submarine

Weapon of war

During the Civil War (1861–65), one side offered money to submarine
inventors who could sink enemy navy ships. The *H.L. Hunley* submarine,
named after the man who paid for it, sank the USS *Housatonic* in 1864
by ramming an explosive harpoon into its side. After this success the
H.L. Hunley also sank, but nobody knows why.

This illustration shows the inside
of the *H.L. Hunley*. The crew of
eight turned the **propeller** fast
enough to ram enemy ships.

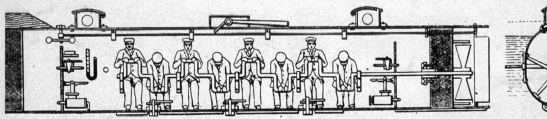

15

1797—Robert Fulton
invents the *Nautilus*

1790   1800

SUBMARINES WITH ENGINES

Objects move forward through water when the **thrust** (the force moving them forward) is stronger than the **drag**. Early submarines were slow because sailors could not turn the **propellers** fast enough to create a strong thrust. This changed when people invented engines to create more thrust. Today, powerful engines turn giant propellers to thrust submarines fast through the water.

Air power

The *Diver*, invented in 1863 by Charles Burn and Simon Bourgeois, was the first submarine with an engine. The engine used **compressed air**, which is air forced into a small space, for power. Air moved fast from air tanks into a tube-shaped cylinder. This pushed on a piston (a type of plunger) inside. When the piston moved, it turned a **crankshaft** connected to a propeller. The engine had several cylinders with pistons that together spun the propeller fast.

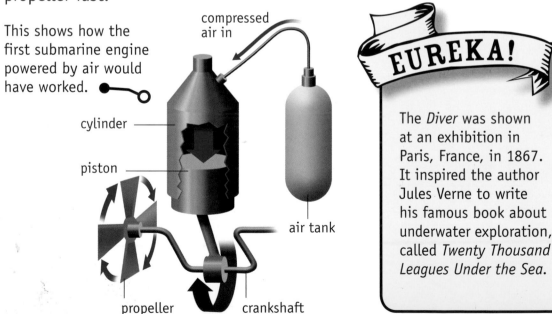

This shows how the first submarine engine powered by air would have worked.

compressed air in

cylinder

piston

air tank

propeller   crankshaft

EUREKA!

The *Diver* was shown at an exhibition in Paris, France, in 1867. It inspired the author Jules Verne to write his famous book about underwater exploration, called *Twenty Thousand Leagues Under the Sea*.

The first torpedoes

In 1866 Robert Whitehead invented **torpedoes**. These are underwater weapons that allow submarines to attack enemies safely from a distance. The first torpedoes were long tubes packed with explosives. They had compressed air inside that thrust them forward when it was released. Today, torpedoes have engines inside them and they can steer themselves toward their targets.

This illustration shows a modern submarine launching a torpedo.

Electric submarine

In a **steam engine**, coal is burned to heat water. The hot water produces steam that moves pistons and turns wheels or **propellers**. People found that it was not good to use steam engines inside submarines because burning coal used up the **oxygen** that sailors needed to breathe, and made lots of heat and smoke.

In 1897 John Philip Holland invented the *Holland VI* submarine, which used **battery** power. A battery is a store of electricity. Electricity from the batteries made an electric motor turn the propeller. The *Holland VI* also had an engine that burned gasoline to power the propeller. Sailors ran this engine when the submarine was near the surface, to move the submarine and to recharge its batteries.

This *Holland VI* submarine belonged to the U.S. Navy.

John Philip Holland (1840–1914)

John Philip Holland was an Irish schoolteacher who spent half his life inventing submarines. His sixth submarine, the *Holland VI*, was the most successful. It held six sailors and could travel 50 kilometers (30 miles) underwater before the batteries needed to be recharged. The submarine could stay underwater for 40 hours, but it was very cramped onboard. Holland sold many bigger and faster versions of the *Holland VI* to the British, Japanese, Russian, and U. S. navies. One of Holland's last inventions was a machine designed to help sailors escape from damaged submarines.

19

1863—The *Diver* is the first submarine with an engine, powered by **compressed air**

1864—The Spanish submarine *Ictineo II* is the first submarine to use steam power at the surface and a different chemical engine underwater

1864—The *H.L. Hunley* is successfully used in the Civil War

1866—Robert Whitehead invents the **torpedo**

1870   1880

Nuclear submarines

During World War I (1914–18) and World War II (1939–45) all submarines used electric motors. In 1954 the U.S. Navy launched the first nuclear submarine. The *Nautilus* had a **steam engine**, but the heat to make the steam came from a **nuclear reactor**. This is a sealed container filled with special metals that keep releasing heat for years.

Nuclear submarines could go faster and farther than electric ones. They did not need to come to the surface to recharge **batteries** or return to land to get more fuel. The trouble with nuclear reactors is that they are very expensive and dangerous if they develop problems. Today, most big navy submarines are nuclear, but many smaller submarines are still electric.

Here, a nuclear submarine surfaces through Arctic sea ice.

EUREKA!

In 1958 the *Nautilus* became the first submarine to travel under the thick sea ice of the North Pole, from the Atlantic to the Pacific oceans. The submarine stayed underwater without surfacing for a distance of about 3,000 kilometers (1,800 miles).

1897—John Holland builds the gasoline and electric *Holland VI*

Submarine comforts

Modern nuclear submarines can weigh more than 24,000 tonnes (23,500 tons)—as much as 200 blue whales—and can carry 150 sailors. They are much more comfortable for sailors to live in than earlier submarines. They have bedrooms, showers, and toilets, and a restaurant open 24 hours a day. They have special machines to turn seawater into drinking water and to keep the air fresh.

These sailors are relaxing in the cramped spaces of the nuclear submarine NR-1.

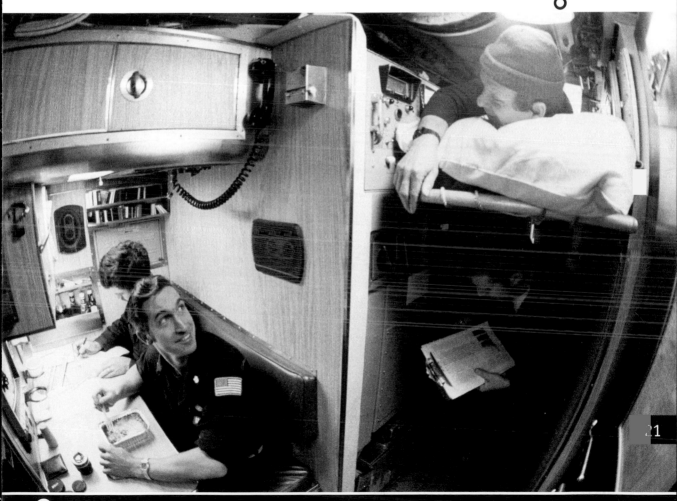

1902—Simon Lake invents the modern submarine **periscope**

EXPLORING THE OCEANS

The deeper a submarine goes underwater, the more water there is above it. The weight of this water pressing down is called **water pressure**. To go really deep underwater, inventors had to make submarines that could survive the enormous water pressure there.

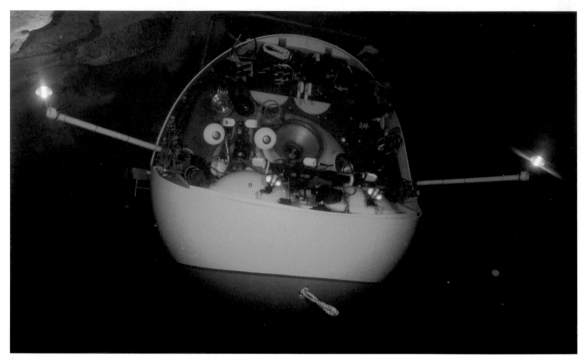

Water pressure at a few dozen feet deep could force in water through gaps in the **hulls** of early submarines. Their hulls could collapse and windows could crack. Many of today's submarines have hulls made of very strong steel that is more than 15 centimeters (6 inches) thick, and windows made of even thicker glass or plastic. Now submarines can dive hundreds of feet deep into the ocean.

Here, the *Mir-2* is about to reach the Mid-Atlantic Ridge, on the bottom of the Atlantic Ocean.

The deepest submarine

Only seven submarines with people inside have ever dived deeper than 3 kilometers (1.8 miles). In 1960 the *Trieste*, invented by Auguste Piccard, went down to almost 11 kilometers (7 miles) deep. The people inside sat in a small metal sphere that was part of the hull. This shape is best at coping with high water pressure, which at that depth was like having 50 jumbo jets sitting on top of the submarine!

Here, the *Trieste* is being lowered into the sea.

EUREKA!

In January 1960, Jacques Piccard and Donald Walsh reached the bottom of the Marianas Trench near the Phillippines in the *Trieste*. The trench is the deepest point of all the oceans.

1948—Hyman Rickover develops a small **nuclear reactor** that is designed to power a submarine

1953—Dimitri Rebikoff invents the first **ROV** submarine

1954—USS *Nautilus* is the first nuclear submarine

1950

1960

Looking above

From inside a submarine, sailors can look above the water for enemy ships by using a **periscope**. Periscopes are long tubes with angled mirrors inside. Light from the outside hits the top mirror, reflecting down through the periscope and off the lower mirror.

Early periscopes were not very good. In 1902 U.S. inventor Simon Lake created a better version with **lenses** inside. Lenses are discs of glass that help to enlarge and focus what sailors can see through a periscope. The periscopes on today's nuclear submarines have digital cameras that can show the view on a computer screen.

This diagram shows how a periscope is used for looking above the surface of the water.

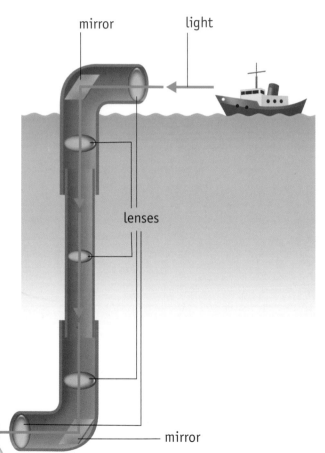

mirror

light

lenses

mirror

1960— The *Trieste* carries out the deepest manned dive in history

1964—The magnetic sea engine is invented

1981—The first Typhoon class nuclear submarine, the biggest ever submarine, is launched by the Russian navy

1960

1970

1980

Submarines without people

In 1953 an inventor named Dimitri Rebikoff made the first robot submarine. It was called POODLE and did not need people on board to control it. Rebikoff operated his machine by sending computer instructions along a cable from a ship on the surface. Machines such as this are called Remote Operated Vehicles (**ROVs**). ROVs are usually small so they can explore shipwrecks and other places that larger submarines cannot.

EUREKA!

In 1986 Robert Ballard used the ROV *Jason Jr.* to take the first photographs inside the world's most famous shipwreck, the *Titanic*. This ship sank to the bottom of the Atlantic Ocean after crashing into an iceberg in 1912.

Here, ROV *Jason Jr.* can be seen exploring the *Titanic* shipwreck.

1986—ROV *Jason Jr.* takes the first photographs inside the *Titanic* shipwreck

1990   2000

INTO THE FUTURE

Submarines have changed a lot since they were first invented 400 years ago. Today, submarines are bigger, more **streamlined**, and faster. They can dive deeper, travel farther, and stay underwater longer. In what ways could submarines change in the future?

Some modern submarines are massive. Here, the newly built HMS *Astute* submarine is being transported to the sea.

No propellers

In the future, submarines may move around without **propellers**. Some may pump jets of water backward to make themselves **thrust** forward. Others may use special **magnets** to make a jet of water thrust them forward. In 2007 James Tangorra invented a robot fish fin that could make an **ROV** thrust forward, change direction, and also hover on the spot. It uses less electricity than propellers.

2004—Rob Innes builds the *Seabreacher* submarine

2008—The *Super Falcon* submarine is launched

2000   2010   2020

Underwater tourism

The *Super Falcon* submarine, invented by Graham Hawkes in 2008, is built for two people. It is shaped like a small fighter aircraft. It is light, fast, and has long wings that help it to dive. On some coasts, such as those in Hawaii, there are already large submarines that take tourists on trips underwater. In the future, tourists may stay at underwater hotels and explore the oceans in their own personal submarines like the *Super Falcon*.

The *Seabreacher* personal submarine can roll and even leap out of the water.

EUREKA!

Thomas Rowe, who loved to surf, designed a robot dolphin submarine after watching dolphins playing in the waves. His student Rob Innes later built the *Seabreacher* submarine, based on Rowe's designs.

27

TIMELINE

3000 BCE
Greek divers use hollow straws to breathe while underwater

332 BCE
Alexander the Great uses a diving bell

1578 CE
William Bourne publishes a book called *Inventions and Devices*. It contains his ideas for how to make a working submarine.

1862
The USS *Alligator* is the longest, most advanced submarine in the world

1852
Lodner Phillips invents a submarine **propeller** that can angle to steer the machine

1797
Robert Fulton invents the *Nautilus*

1863
The *Diver* is the first submarine with an engine, powered by **compressed air**

1864
The Spanish submarine *Ictineo II* is the first steam-powered submarine

1864
The *H.L. Hunley* is successfully used in the Civil War

1866
Robert Whitehead invents the **torpedo**

2008
The *Super Falcon* submarine is launched

2004
Rob Innes builds the *Seabreacher* submarine

1986
ROV *Jason Jr.* takes the first photographs inside the *Titanic* shipwreck

1981
The first Typhoon class nuclear submarine, the biggest ever submarine, is launched by the Russian navy

1620
The *Drebbel* is the world's first successful submarine

1634
A French priest and scientist named Marin Mersenne writes that submarines should be made of copper and shaped like long cylinders to move easily through the water

1653
The *Rotterdam Boat* is invented but never works

1776
David Bushnell invents and demonstrates his *Turtle* submarine. It is the first submarine able to move independently above and below the water.

1729
Nathaniel Symons builds a submarine that can change its **volume**

1680
Giovanni Borelli invents the **ballast tank** to change the weight and **density** of a submarine

1897
John Philip Holland builds the gasoline and electric *Holland VI*

1902
Simon Lake invents the modern submarine **periscope**

1948
Hyman Rickover develops a small **nuclear reactor** to power a submarine

1964
The magnetic sea engine is invented

1960
The *Trieste* carries out the deepest manned dive in history

1954
USS *Nautilus* is the first nuclear submarine

1953
Dimitri Rebikoff invents the first **ROV** submarine

INDEX